READ *it,* SEE *it,* SAY *it,* SING *it!*

Knowing and Loving the Bible

Hunter Beless

illustrated by Hsulynn Pang

B&H kids
Brentwood TN

To Hadley, Davy, and Bo,
my favorite Scripture memory partners.
Keep hiding God's Word in your hearts!

Text copyright © 2021 by Hunter Beless.
Illustrations copyright © 2021 by B&H Publishing Group.
Published in 2022 by B&H Publishing Group, Brentwood, Tennessee.
ISBN: 978-1-0877-5250-1
Unless noted otherwise, Scripture quotations are taken from The Holy Bible,
English Standard Version®, ESV® Text Edition: 2016. Copyright © 2001 by Crossway Bibles,
a publishing ministry of Good News Publishers.
Scripture quotations marked CSB are taken from the Christian Standard Bible®,
Copyright © 2017 by Holman Bible Publishers. Used by permission. Christian Standard Bible®
and CSB® are federally registered trademarks of Holman Bible Publishers.
Dewey Decimal Classification: CE
SUBHD: BIBLE—USE / CHRISTIAN LIFE / SPIRITUAL LIFE
Printed in Shenzhen, Guangdong, China, in May 2023
4 5 6 7 8 9 10 · 27 26 25 24 23

Endorsements

"There can be no more important thing in a child's life than for them to grow to know, understand, and love not only the Word of God but also the saving grace of the God of the Word. *Read It, See It, Say It, Sing It!* puts a tool in the parents' hands that helps them encourage this in their children's lives. I highly recommend this book to moms and dads who want to pass their love for God and His Word to another generation."

Paul David Tripp, author of *New Morning Mercies: A Daily Gospel Devotional* and *Parenting: 14 Gospel Principles That Can Radically Change Your Family*

"Read It, See it, Say it, Sing It! is a helpful reminder to all ages that we will grow when we rehearse the truth of God's Word. This resource is a treasured gift for not only your children's hearts and minds but yours, too!"

Ruth Chou Simons, mom to six boys, founder of GraceLaced, and bestselling author

"Hunter skillfully engages kids with a rhyme that sticks and gets them excited about the value of God's Word. We can't wait to read this with our own kids, using it as a tool to help them incorporate Scripture in every part of life! In a world of filler words, kids need a rhyme like this in their heads and hearts."

Emily Jensen & Laura Wifler, cofounders of Risen Motherhood

"Hunter has given us a beautiful and exciting children's book about the immeasurable value of God's Word. Gorgeous illustrations and Bible verses fill this excellent book, which very clearly articulates the gospel message for kids and adults alike. I'm thrilled to know many families will catch on to the joy of Scripture memory through Hunter's work!"

Quina Aragon, author of the children's books, *Love Made: A Story of God's Overflowing, Creative Heart* and *Love Gave: A Story of God's Greatest Gift*

"This delightful, imaginative, engaging book is one children and those who read to them will enjoy hearing over and over. And each time it is read, the wonder and beauty of God's Word will go deeper and deeper."

Susan Hunt, former Coordinator of Women's Ministries for the PCA and author of several books for women and children

"An absolutely beautiful book written by someone who lives out its message. This is a must-have for any parent trying to raise children who love Jesus and His Word."

Jerrad Lopes, founder of dadtired.com, host of the Dad Tired podcast, and author of *Stop Behaving* and *Dad Tired and Loving it: Stumbling Your Way to Spiritual Leadership*

Luke 21:33

Have you heard of the
special book God gave to us?
If not, this is something
that we should discuss!

This book is the Bible.
It's timeless and true.
It's God's written Word—
both for me and for you.

Psalm 19:7

Psalm 119:162

We READ it out loud, so
we hear what God says.

We SEE it to crave it and eat it like bread.

We SAY it to hide its truths
deep in our hearts.

We SING it so others can come and take part.

READ it, SEE it, SAY it, SING it!

We live by God's Word because we believe it.

But who is the hero of this special story?
It's God's Son named Jesus. He shows us God's glory.

The Bible's whole message—beginning to end—
is Jesus can save us from death and from sin!

Hebrews 1:1-3

Romans 6:23

Luke 24:27

And the Word became flesh and dwelt among us, and we have seen his glory,

glory as of the only Son from the Father, full of grace and truth.
—John 1:14

"What's sin?" you may ask. It's a heart gone astray.
It's ignoring God's Word, His will, and His way.

But God forgives us when we turn from our sin, because Jesus lived, died, and then rose again!

If we say we have no sin, we deceive ourselves, and the truth is not in us. If we confess our sins, he is faithful and just to forgive us our sins and to cleanse us from all unrighteousness. —1 John 1:8-9

2 Corinthians 5:21

READ *it,*

Matthew 5:17

SEE *it,*

Your word is a lamp to my feet and a light to my path.
—Psalm 119:105

We treasure God's Word because JESUS is in it!

We gobble God's words like the very best food.
They comfort our hearts when we're in a bad mood.

READ it, SEE it, SAY it, SING it!
We feast on God's Word every day
'cause we need it.

Psalm 19:9-10

Matthew 4:4

Your words were found, and I ate them, and your words became to me a joy and the delight of my heart, for I am called by your name, O Lord, God of hosts. ~Jeremiah 15:16

Ezekiel 3:1-3

15

When we put God's truth
right in front of our eyes,
we draw close to Jesus
as we memorize.

READ it, SEE it, SAY it, SING it!
We study the Bible
and gladly receive it.

We talk about it when we sit and we rise.
Reciting, repeating it helps us be wise.

You shall teach them of them when you sit in and when you lie down,

Psalm 1:1-2

READ it, SEE it, SAY it, SING it!
We remember God's Word
so that we never leave it.

diligently to your children, and shall talk your house, and when you walk by the way, and when you rise.—Deuteronomy 6:7

Romans 10:17

Deuteronomy 30:14

We hear from the Bible then sing with each other.
We share about Jesus and love one another.

READ it, SEE it, SAY it, SING it!

Psalm 34:3

Romans 11:33–36

20

Serve the Lord with gladness!
Come into His presence with singing!
–Psalm 100:2

We live out God's Word
and pray He'll help us keep it!

James 1:22

21

Psalm 147:3

When we're jealous or worried,
excited or mad,

Matthew 11:28

Since then we have a great high priest who has passed through the heavens, Jesus, the Son of God, let us hold fast our confession.

when we're hurting or lonely,
delighted or sad. . .

1 Peter 5:7

For we do not have a high priest who is unable to sympathize with our weaknesses, but one who in every respect has been tempted as we are, yet without sin.
—Hebrews 4:14-15

Psalm 145:18

LOVE Joy
PEACE
Patience KINDNESS
GOODNESS Faithfulness
GENTLENESS
SELF-CONTROL

God's Word gives us hope, meets us right where we are,
and shows that our God isn't distant or far.

1 Thessalonians 2:13

24

READ it, SEE it, SAY it, SING it!

Romans 15:4

God speaks through the Bible.
That's why we draw near it.

25

God uses His Word to change us from within.
Our hearts long for Him, and that helps us fight sin.

Psalm 119:11

For the word of God is living and active, sharper than any two-edged sword, piercing to the division of soul and of spirit, of joints and of marrow, and discerning the thoughts and intentions of the heart. –Hebrews 4:12

Proverbs 30:5

READ it, SEE it, SAY it, SING it!

We put sin to death by the sword of the Spirit!

Galatians 5:16

God's Word changes EVERYTHING—heads, hearts, and hands.
We obey God's truth, and His kingdom expands.

John 18:36

John 17:17

I am the Alpha and the Omega, the first and the last,
the beginning and the end.—Revelation 22:13

The story of Scripture points us to one thing:
That JESUS can save us, and He is our King!

Revelation 19:16

At the end of the day,
when we're cozy in bed,
we delight in and wonder
at all that God says.

This Book of the Law shall not depart from your mouth, but you shall meditate on it day and night, so that you may be careful to do according to all that is written in it. For then you will make your way prosperous, and then you will have good success. –Joshua 1:8

Colossians 3:16

Psalm 4:8

We READ and we SEE and we SAY and we SING, to worship and praise God in everything!

REMEMBER: And he [Jesus] said to him, "You shall love the Lord your God with all your heart and with all your soul and with all your mind."–Matthew 22:37

READ: Deuteronomy 6:4-9

Someone once asked Jesus to share the greatest commandment of all. Jesus then said the most important thing we can do is love God more than anything else (Matthew 22:37). READ it, SEE it, SAY it, SING it is a method that we can use to remember to love God with everything we've got— Deuteronomy chapter six style! Here's how you can do that today:

READ it: Reading the Bible reminds us that we live by every word that comes from the mouth of God (Matthew 4:4). Just like our favorite food, we gobble up God's words because they're sweeter than honey (Psalm 119:103) and in them, we find life (Deuteronomy 32:47). Together, we can read the Bible and memorize verses that will help us delight in the life Jesus offers us!

SEE it: God told His people, the Israelites, to put His commands between their eyes and to write them on the doorposts of their houses and gates (Deuteronomy 6:8-9). That might sound a bit extreme, but like the Israelites, we place God's words where we can see them easily so we can remember them wherever we go! Written reminders, pictures and symbols, and hand motions will help us quickly recall passages we are hiding in our hearts.

SAY it: God gave us His Word so that we can hear it, believe it, and respond in faith (Romans 10:17). But we fail to trust God every day, which shows us just how much we need His grace! By reciting Scripture repeatedly, we remember who God is and what He has done for us through His Son, Jesus (Romans 6:23; 2 Corinthians 5:21). As we repeat God's promises out loud, we praise Jesus, the founder and perfecter of our faith (Hebrews 12:2).

SING it: We sing God's Word to tell Him how much we love Him, and doing so encourages others to love Him too (Romans 15:6-7). Adding music and melody to Scripture can help us memorize the words and easily remind us of God's truths. By creating a catchy tune or cadence, or by setting the verse to a rhythmic beat, we share the good news about Jesus wherever we go, just as He commanded us to do (Matthew 28:18-20).

Example:

READ it: Read Matthew 22:37 aloud.

SEE it: Use the following hand motions or draw a picture to remember the words Jesus said in Matthew 22:37: **LOVE**: make a heart with your hands; **GOD**: point up to the sky; **HEART**: place your hands over your heart; **SOUL**: bring your hands from your belly to your chest; **MIND**: point to your head.

SAY it: Repeat Matthew 22:37 aloud while doing the hand motions 3-5 times.

SING it: Sing or chant the verse together, emphasizing the emboldened words: "**YOU** shall **LOVE** the **LORD** your **GOD** with **ALL** your **HEART** and with **ALL** your **SOUL** and with **ALL** your **MIND**."